Where'd They Get That Idea?

Issues and Ideas in Science and Mathematics

Volume I

STUDENT GUIDE

by Howard Zeiderman

TOUCHSTONES
DISCUSSION PROJECT

About Touchstones Discussion Project

The Touchstones Discussion Project is a nonprofit organization founded on the belief that all people can benefit from the listening, speaking, thinking, and interpersonal skills gained by engaging in active, focused discussions. Since 1984, Touchstones has helped millions of students and others develop and improve these skills in school, work, and life. For more information about the Touchstones Discussion Project, visit www.touchstones.org.

Special Thanks to Corbis for donation of the following images used in the cover design:
ISBN:1-878-46149-4

Abstract background:	Image courtesy of Corbis, Image ID 8731 © Lawrence Manning/CORBIS
X-ray of human head:	Image courtesy of Corbis, Image ID MED2052 © Royalty-Free/CORBIS
Nebula:	Image courtesy of Corbis, Image ID RR013023 © Roger Ressmeyer/CORBIS
Lightning bolts:	Image courtesy of Corbis, Image ID SCH028 © Royalty-Free/CORBIS
Great White Shark:	Image courtesy of Corbis, Image ID SHK001 © Royalty-Free/CORBIS
Pyramid of Kukulkan:	Image courtesy of Corbis, Image ID WTR090 © Royalty-Free/CORBIS

Cover design by Daniel P. Sullivan

Table of Contents

Lesson 1   Getting Started 1
The Orientation Class

Lesson 2   *Money Makes Cares*, a Tale from China .5

Lesson 3   How Long Could You Observe a Smelly Fish? 9
Studying a Fish, S.H. Scudder

Lesson 4   Are These Figures the Same? 15
Euclid's Classification of Triangles

Lesson 5   Why Does a Ball Keep Moving After You Throw It? 23
Mathematical Principles of Natural Philosophy, Sir Isaac Newton

Lesson 6   How Straight Is Straight? 27
Definitions of a Straight Line, Various Authors

Lesson 7   How Does a Scientist Think? 31
The Making of a Scientist, Richard Feynmann

Lesson 8   Do You Like Mathematics? 35
Two Different Kinds of Minds, Blaise Pascal

Lesson 9   Does the Universe Ever End? 39
On the Nature of Things, Lucretius

Lesson 10   Why Do We Study Math? 43
The Arithmetic, Nicomachus of Gerasa
A Conversation Between Abraham Lincoln and J.P. Gulliver, 1860

Lesson 11   Symmetry: Can You Prove It? 47
A Geometrical Theorem, Euclid

Lesson 12   Should Scientists Experiment on Animals? 51
Introduction to Experimental Medicine, C. Bernard

Lesson 13   Is That Reason Enough? 55
Letter to Dr. Clarke, G. W. Leibniz

Lesson 14   How Big Is Infinity? 59
Physics, Aristotle

Lesson 15   Why Do I Have To Prove It? 63
Two Proofs of the Same Truth

Lesson 16   Will the Sun Rise Tomorrow? 67
"Common Ideas" from *The Elements*, Euclid

Lesson 17   Are Scientists Responsible for Their Inventions? 71
The Value of Science, Henri Poincaré

Lesson 18   Do Triangles Really Exist? 75
The Republic, Plato
Geometry and Experience, Albert Einstein

The Orientation Class

You, your classmates, and your teacher are about to begin a class which differs in some ways from your regular classes. The purpose of this class is to enable you to gain certain skills that will help you profit more from your regular classes. The new class is a discussion class. You will be talking to one another as well as to your teacher. We are all familiar with discussions because we have all discussed problems, feelings, opinions, and experiences with friends and relatives throughout our lives. However, the discussions you will have in this class differ in some ways from your previous experiences.

Unlike your regular classes

a) everyone sits in a circle;

b) the teacher is a member of the group and will help, but isn't an authority with the correct answers;

c) there is no hand raising, instead everyone will learn how to run the discussion;

d) there is no preparation.

Unlike discussions which happen outside of class with friends and relatives

a) discussions involve everyone in the class, your friends as well as students you don't know very well;

b) discussions are about readings from the Touchstones book and not just our own concerns and experiences;

c) discussions occur once a week at a scheduled time, begin with a question asked by the teacher, and end when the teacher decides or when the bell rings.

Because of these differences, everyone must follow certain ground rules. These are listed on the next page.

Ground Rules

1. **Read the text carefully.** In Touchstones discussions your opinions are important, but these opinions are your thoughts about the text.

2. **Listen to what others say and don't interrupt.** A discussion cannot occur if you don't listen carefully to what people say.

3. **Speak clearly.** For others to respond to your opinions, everyone must be able to hear and understand you.

4. **Give others your respect.** A discussion is a cooperative exchange of ideas and not an argument or a debate. You may become excited and wish to share your ideas, but don't talk privately to your neighbor. In a Touchstones class, you will talk publicly for the whole class.

Goals
What you can gain from Touchstones Discussion classes

You will learn

a) listen better to what others say,

b) explain your own ideas,

c) speak and work with others whether you know them or not,

d) receive correction and criticism from others,

e) ask about what you don't understand,

f) admit when you're wrong,

g) think about questions for which the answers are uncertain,

h) learn from others,

i) teach others,

j) teach yourself, and

k) become more aware of how others see you.

Worksheet #1

Individual Work

Complete the following questions on your own.

1. Which Ground Rule do you think will be the hardest for the class to follow? Why?

_____   _____

_____

_____

_____

_____

_____

2. Which Ground Rule will be hardest for you to follow? Why?

_____

_____

_____

_____

_____

_____

Complete question 3 after the discussion.

3. Choose one or two of the goals (a-k) that you would like to achieve through this program. Write their letters here.

_____

_____

Small Group Work

I. The chairperson of your group is responsible for organizing the group, making sure everyone participates, and presenting the group's answers to the whole class. The secretary is responsible for recording your group's answers. The participants are responsible for being cooperative and helping to make sure the group work gets done.

II. Form a circle with your chairs to make sure each person in the group is included.

III. Each person in the group should share what he or she wrote down for #1.

IV. Everyone in the group should decide on the one ground rule that will be the most difficult for the class to follow. Write your group's choice here. _____
Why did your group choose this ground rule?

_____

_____

_____

_____

_____

_____

_____

_____

_____

_____

_____

_____

_____

Money Makes Cares
A Tale from China

Chen was a rich man who lived many years ago. He had so much money that he was always busy investing it, lending it, and paying taxes. From morning to night he never had a moment's peace. He had little time to eat—he never had dinner until late at night.

His wife pitied him for all the worries he had, and kept saying to him, "Look after yourself. Please don't work yourself to death." Chen agreed with her, but he did not know how to stop working.

His neighbor, Ti, was very poor. He and his wife together earned just enough to keep themselves alive. Ti was a good workman, and it was usually evening before he stopped work. Then he went home, gave his wife the money he had earned, and worried about nothing else. If he was in a good mood, he sang songs. That was his only amusement; at least it didn't cost any money.

The sounds of Ti singing and of Ti and his wife talking could be heard in Chen's house. But Chen was too busy going through his checks and bills to pay attention. His wife, however, was saddened by the happy sounds.

When Chen finally sat down for his evening meal, the sounds from Ti's house could still be heard. Chen's wife said to him, "Listen, Ti sounds so happy, although he is so poor. We are so rich, and yet we are never happy."

"Have you never heard the proverb, 'The penniless man has plenty of time'?" asked Chen. "He can be happy because he is poor. It would be quite easy to make him quit singing. We need only give him some money." "If you do that, he will become even happier," answered his wife. "Wait a little while," said Chen. "If you still hear him singing, I will admit I was wrong."

Next morning Chen invited Ti to his house and gave him a great deal of money. Never having dreamed of such a gift, Ti could only stammer out, "Many thanks for your kindness." He took the money and rushed home excited to tell his wife all that had happened. Now he no longer went to work. He did nothing but wonder how to use the money. He couldn't decide. Now when he came home, he was late for dinner and gulped it down quickly. Naturally, he had no time for singing or playing. He couldn't sleep at night thinking about the money.

Chen and his wife listened carefully to hear what their neighbor Ti did. There was no sound of singing. "Was I right?" Chen asked his wife. His wife smiled and admitted he was right.

For two nights Ti could get no sleep. On the morning of the third day the God of Luck appeared before him and said, "Money makes cares. Think of that, and bother no more about it."

Ti understood and, leaping out of bed, he hurried and gave the money back to Chen.

Ti felt as though a weight had been taken off his heart. He went home and slept like a baby. The next day he went out to work and, in the evening, the sound of singing and playing was once again heard coming from Ti's house.

Worksheet #2

 Individual Work

1. List below three ways in which you believe possessing a huge amount of money would make you happy.

   a. _____

   _____

   _____

   b. _____

   _____

   _____

   c. _____

   _____

   _____

2. List below three ways in which you believe having a huge amount of money would give you problems and make you unhappy.

   a. _____

   _____

   _____

   b. _____

   _____

   _____

   c. _____

   _____

   _____

6

Where'd They Get That Idea? Volume 1

Small Group Work

I.   The chairperson of your group is responsible for organizing the group, making sure everyone participates, and presenting those answers to the whole class. The secretary is responsible for recording your group's answers. The participants are responsible for being cooperative and helping to make sure the group work gets done.

II. Form a circle with your chairs to make sure each person in the group is included.

III. Compare your individual answers to the questions above.

IV. In the space below, the secretary should write down as many suggestions as your group can think of on how to prevent the unhappiness or problems that wealth might cause without getting rid of it as Ti does.

_____

_____

_____

_____

_____

_____

_____

_____

_____

_____

_____

_____

_____

_____

Lesson 3

Worksheet #3-A

Individual Work

     We have all had the experience of looking at something but not really seeing what was there. How many times have you looked for something you lost but didn't see it even though it was right in front of you? How many things are there to see on the school grounds which you have never noticed? Paying attention to what is around us seems like the easiest thing to do. But really paying attention is one of the hardest things in the world to do. You have to train yourself to do it. Learning to pay attention, to really observe, is the beginning of all science. This is especially true of biology. Biologists are interested in the ways that things which are very similar differ from one another. For example, how different can the leaves from one tree be? How different are the reactions of different patients to the same medicine? Is this spot on this person's arm normal or something to worry about? In this class we will be doing some exercises to help you become better observers of the world around you.

     Look around your classroom and write down three things you have not noticed before. For example, how many lights are there on the ceiling? Compare what you have seen with the other students in the class.

1. _____

  _____

  _____

  _____

2. _____

  _____

  _____

  _____

3. _____

  _____

  _____

  _____

Studying A Fish
by S. H. Scudder

It was more than fifteen years ago (from 1874) that I entered the laboratory of Professor Agassiz and told him I had enrolled my name as a student of natural history.

"When do you wish to begin?" he asked.

"Now," I replied.

This seemed to please him, and with an energetic "Very well!" he reached from a shelf a huge jar of specimens in yellow alcohol.

"Take this fish," he said, "and look at it; soon I will ask what you have seen."

In ten minutes I had seen all that I thought could be seen in that fish, and started in search of the Professor.

On my return, I learned that Professor Agassiz had gone, and would not return for several hours. Slowly I drew forth that hideous fish, and with a feeling of desperation again looked at it. I might not use a magnifying-glass; instruments of all kinds were not allowed. My two hands, my two eyes, and the fish: it seemed a most limited field. I pushed my finger down its throat to feel how sharp the teeth were. I began to count the scales in the different rows. At last a happy thought struck me—I would draw the fish; and now with surprise I began to discover new features in the creature. Just then the Professor returned.

"That is right," he said, "a pencil is one of the best eyes."

With these encouraging words, he added: "Well, what is it like?"

He listened attentively to my brief rehearsal of the structure of parts whose names were still unknown to me:

"You have not looked very carefully; why," he continued more earnestly, "you haven't even seen one of the most obvious features of the animal, which is as plainly before your eyes as the fish itself; look again, look again!" and he left me to my misery.

The afternoon passed quickly and toward its close the Professor inquired:

"Do you see it yet?"

"No," I replied, "I am certain I do not, but I see how little I saw before."

"That is next best," he said, earnestly, "but I won't hear you now. Put away your fish and go home; perhaps you will be ready with a better answer in the morning. I will examine you before you look at the fish."

The friendly greeting from the Professor the next morning was reassuring; here was a man who seemed to be quite as anxious as I that I should see for myself what he saw.

"Do you perhaps mean," I asked, "that the fish has symmetrical sides with paired organs, each side the same as the other?"

He was thoroughly pleased. "Of course! of course!" repaid the wakeful hours of the previous night.

I dared to ask what I should do next.

"Oh, look at your fish!" he said, and left me again to my own devices. In a little more than an hour he returned, and heard my new catalogue.

"That is good, that is good!" he repeated, "but that is not all. Go on." And so for three long days he placed that fish before my eyes forbidding me to look at anything else or to use any artificial aid. "Look, look, look," was his repeated command.

This was the best scientific lesson I ever had—a lesson whose influence has extended far. It was a gift the Professor has left to me as he has left it to many others, of inestimable value, which we could not buy, with which we cannot part.

Worksheet #3-B

 Small Group Work

I. Draw the leaf in front of you as carefully as you can. Make a list of one or two important features that would distinguish your leaf from any other leaf.

Important Features

a. _____

_____

_____

_____

b. _____

_____

_____

_____

II.   Now draw a picture of a second leaf from the same type of tree. List some important ways that the two leaves are different. Compare with the other students in your small group.

Ways Leaves are Different

a. _____

_____

_____

_____

b. _____

_____

_____

_____

Journal

Choose one question, check its box, and answer it below.

❑ How does this story relate to your own drawings and observations of the leaves?

❑ What does the professor mean when he says that "a pencil is one of the best eyes?"

❑ How is the observation of the fish the best scientific lesson for the author?

❑ Why did the Professor not allow the author to use artificial aids?

Lesson 4

Worksheet #4-A

Work In Pairs

We have all said that two things or people were exactly the same or at least very similar to one another. Sometimes we feel that family members are very different but that two friends are just alike. Sometimes people, even when they look very different, are mistaken for one another because they are so similar in their opinions or behavior. A very close friend of mine and I are often called by one another's names. Perhaps that has also happened to you. Things and people could be similar or the same in many different ways. Working in pairs, you will select four things in the room that you feel will be hard to find to be similar. Each pair passes its list to another pair and gets another pair's list. Each must figure out at least one similarity among the four objects, and write this similarity in the space provided at the bottom of the page. An important part of mathematics and science is deciding which things we will group together. Often how we group things will greatly influence how we study them because we begin to concentrate on what they have in common. In today's class we will explore grouping things together and the ways in which we see what geometrical figures have in common.

Look around the room and choose four objects that have something in common but are not obviously related. When you are done, your teacher will ask you to switch lists with another group. You will then have to figure out what their four objects have in common and they will have to figure out what your four objects have in common.

Your List

1. _____

_____

2. _____

_____

3. _____

_____

4. _____

_____

What do these four things have in common?

_____

_____

Worksheet #4-B

Small Group Work

I. Each group will need a pair of scissors. Cut out one set of figures from the handout your teacher gives you.

II. As a group, decide how you would categorize the figures. Divide the figures into at least three different categories, but not more than five categories.

III. List the numbers of the figures in each category and a reason explaining why those figures are in the same category.

Category 1

Figure #'s: _____

Reason: _____

_____

Category 2

Figure #'s: _____

Reason: _____

_____

Category 3

Figure #'s: _____

Reason: _____

_____

Category 4

Figure #'s: _____

Reason: _____

_____

Category 5

Figure #'s: _____

Reason: _____

_____

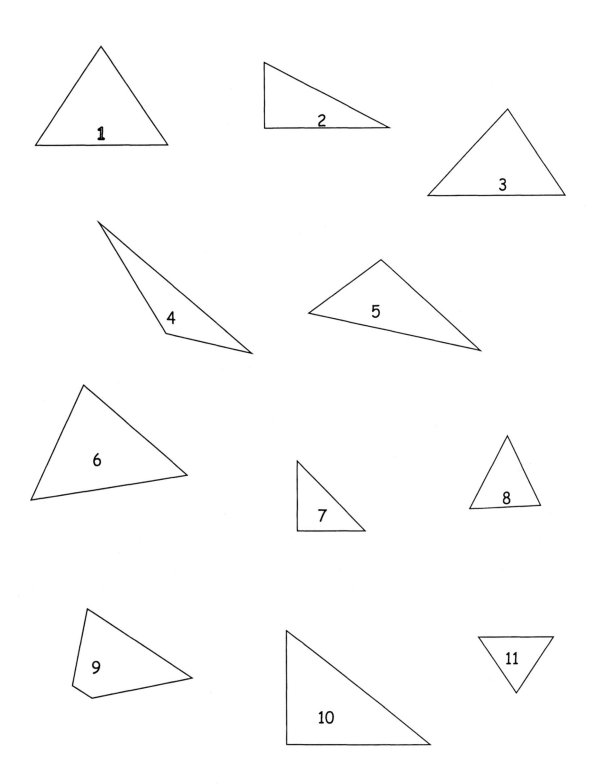

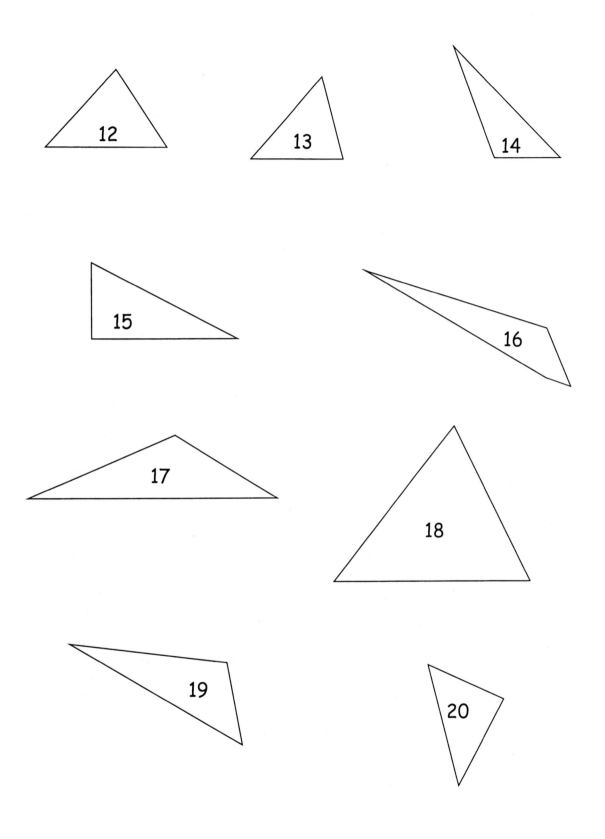

Euclid's Classification of Triangles

Below are the ways the mathematician Euclid would group the figures you have been working with. After each type are the numbers of the triangles that would be in that group. These may be different from what you did. Which method of grouping do you prefer, yours or his?

1. **Equilateral triangles have three sides of equal length.**

   Triangle #1 is the only one in this group.

2. **An isosceles triangle has two sides of equal length.**

   Triangles #7 and #18 are in this group.

3. **Scalene triangles have three sides with different lengths.**

   Triangles #2, #3, #4, #5, #6, #8, #10, #11, #12, #13, #14, #15, #17, #19 and #20 are in this group.

4. **Figures #9 and #16 have four sides and are not triangles.**

Journal

Euclid also groups triangles according to the type of angles they have. An angle that looks like this ($\llcorner$) is called a right angle, a bigger angle is called obtuse, a smaller angle is called acute.

      A) Right Angle   B) Obtuse Angle   C) Acute Angle

A) A **right-angled triangle** has one right angle, an angle measuring 90 degrees.

B) An **obtuse-angled triangle** has an obtuse angle, an angle greater than 90 degrees.

C) An **acute-angled triangle** has all three angles acute, all less than 90 degrees.

Which triangles from Exercise III are right, which obtuse, and which acute? We have started you off with the first answer in each group.

Right: #2, _____

_____

_____

Obtuse: #4, _____

_____

_____

Acute: #1, _____

_____

_____

Worksheet #5

Lesson 5

Individual Work

i

No experience is more common to us than getting tired. After we have been busy all day we all get tired and eventually need to sleep. Though balls and stones don't get tired, they all eventually stop moving. When we throw a ball, it falls to the ground and stops. Our most common experience of seeing something that is moving along is seeing that it will stop. And if we were scientists who had to make up a rule about things that move, we might well decide that our rule is, "something that is moving will come to a stop." In today's class we will explore what our rule should be. Should it be everything in motion will come to rest? Or will an object in motion come to rest only if stopped by something else? And what about a ball that is at rest? Will it remain that way unless something moves it?

Imagine there is only one thing in the whole universe — a ball. Now, imagine you have to decide what rules the ball will obey. **For each of the following two situations, choose which rule you would apply to the ball.**

1. The ball is moving at 10 miles per hour. What will happen?

   ❑ It will eventually come to rest.

   ❑ It will continue to move at 10 miles per hour.

2. The ball is not moving. What will happen?

   ❑ It will start to move.

   ❑ It will remain at rest.

Small Group Work

Form a small group with other students who have answered #1 and #2 the same as you. Discuss reasons for your choices and write them in the space provided below. Also discuss reasons against the other possibilities.

Reasons for your choices:

I. _____

_____

_____

_____

II. _____

_____

_____

_____

III. _____

_____

_____

_____

Mathematical Principles of Natural Philosophy
by I. Newton

Rule 1

A body which is either at rest or in motion with constant speed in a straight line stays that way. It changes its speed or direction only when forced to do so by something else.

If you throw something, it will keep on moving at constant speed in a straight line. However, all bodies are slowed down by air resistance, or pulled downward by the force of gravity. A top would not stop spinning if it were not slowed down by moving through the air. Planets and comets are much bigger and move through space in which there is very little air resistance. They therefore keep their motions, both circular and in a straight line, for a much longer time.

Journal

Explain Newton's reason for believing that a ball at rest and a ball moving at a constant speed are similar. Do you agree with Newton? Why or why not?

_____

_____

_____

_____

_____

_____

_____

_____

_____

_____

_____

_____

_____

_____

_____

_____

_____

_____

_____

_____

_____

_____

26

Where'd They Get That Idea? Volume 1

Worksheet #6

Ever since you were very young, you have probably been drawing pictures. Some of these were of animals or trees, other drawings were of buildings. Surprisingly, when we look at these pictures, we realize that the hardest thing to draw is a perfectly straight line. Since a straight line is the simplest line there is, this might puzzle us. In addition, though it is easy to tell if a line is not straight, it is very hard to tell if a line is perfectly straight even when we draw it with a ruler.

In this class, we will consider four different ways of explaining to someone how we would decide if a line is perfectly straight. You will discuss which way is best or come up with ideas for better ones.

1. Draw a straight line without any help.

2. Draw a straight line using a straight edge, like a ruler or book.

3. Which of the following lines is straighter between points A and B? Circle the one you choose.

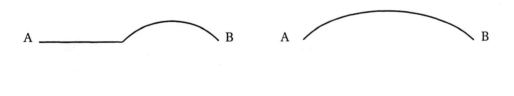

Definitions of a Straight Line
by Various Authors

1. **A straight line is the shortest distance between two points.**

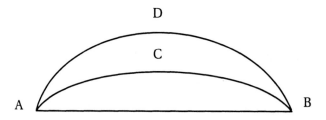

> Line AB is shorter than line ACB and line ACB is shorter than ADB. If line AB is shortest of all lines between A and B, it is perfectly straight.

2. **Imagine a straight line and a curved line drawn between points A and B on a piece of paper. If you spin the paper around points A and B, the curved line moves but the straight line doesn't.**

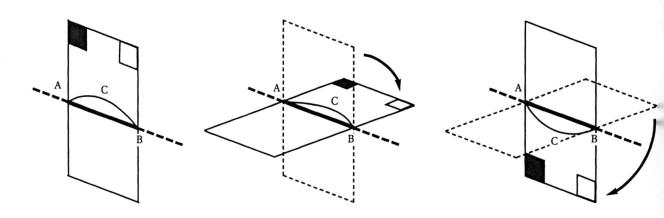

> As the paper turns (follow marks ■ and □), straight line AB doesn't move but curved line ACB does move.

28

Where'd They Get That Idea? Volume 1

3. If you look down a straight line, you only see a point and no other part of that straight line.

    Look along straight line AB

    and all you see is   •

4. Between any two points, such as points A and B, you can draw only one straight line.

    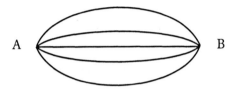

    There is only one possible straight line, AB

5. Two straight lines cannot meet in two points. There are two possibilities for how two straight lines will or will not meet:

    A) 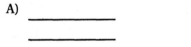   B)

    If two lines meet in two points, then one or both of them must be curved:

Journal

Which definition of a straight line do you prefer? Why?

_____

_____

_____

_____

_____

_____

_____

_____

_____

_____

_____

_____

_____

_____

_____

_____

_____

_____

_____

_____

_____

_____

_____

_____

_____

Worksheet #7

Small Group Work

Imagine that while you were out walking in the woods, you noticed a certain type of small bird. You also saw that all of these birds were continually pecking at their feathers. As a group, try and come up with an explanation for this behavior.

Ⓢ

_____

_____

_____

_____

_____

_____

_____

Individual Work

i

This story about Feynman's walk with his father contains a lot of details, but the details are not equally important. Below is a list of six facts or details in the story. Number them according to how important you think they are where 1 is the most important and 6 is the least important.

____ a. Feynman's father made up names for the bird they observed in several different languages.

____ b. Feynman knew his father's story wasn't exactly true.

____ c. The bird is called a brown-throated thrush.

____ d. Feynman and his father look at the birds and notice there is no particular time when the birds peck their feathers.

____ e. Feynman's father made up a story which connected lice, mites, sugar-like material, and how often birds peck their feathers.

____ f. The story takes place during the summer in the Catskill Mountains.

The Making of a Scientist
by R. Feynman

We used to go to the Catskill Mountains, a place where people from New York City would go in the summer. The fathers would all return to New York to work during the week and come back only for the weekend. On weekends, my father would take me for walks in the woods, and he'd tell me about interesting things that were going on in the woods. When the other mothers saw this, they thought it was wonderful and that the other fathers should take their sons for walks. They tried to work on them, but they didn't get anywhere at first. They wanted my father to take all the kids, but he didn't want to because he had a special relationship with me. So it ended up that the other fathers had to take their children for walks the next weekend.

The next Monday, when the fathers were all back at work, we kids were playing in a field. One kid says to me, "See that bird? What kind of bird is that?"

I said, "I haven't the slightest idea what kind of a bird it is."

He says, "It's a brown-throated thrush. Your father doesn't teach you anything!"

But it was the opposite. He had already taught me more important things.

"See that bird?" my father had said. "It's a Spencer's warbler." (I knew he didn't know the real name and was just making it up.) "Well, in Italian, it's a Chutto Lapottida. In Portuguese, it's a Bom da Pieda. In Chinese, it's a Chung-long-tah, and in Japanese, it's a Latano Tekeda," he said, though I realized these names were also made up by him. "You can know the name of that bird in all the languages of the world, but when you're finished, you'll know absolutely nothing whatever about the bird. All you know are what humans in different places call the bird. So let's look at the bird and see what it's doing— that's what counts." (So, this was an important lesson for me. I learned very early the difference between knowing the name of something and really knowing something about the world.)

"For example, look," he said. "The bird pecks at its feathers all the time. See it walking around, pecking at its feathers?"

"Yeah."

"Why do you think birds peck at their feathers?" he asked.

I said, "Well, maybe they mess up their feathers when they fly, so they're pecking them in order to straighten them out."

"All right," he said. "If that were the case, then they would peck a lot just after they've been flying. But if you're right, after they've been on the ground a while, they wouldn't peck so much any more—you know what I mean?"

"Yeah."

He said, "Let's look and see if they peck more just after they land."

It wasn't hard to tell: there was not much difference between the birds that had been walking around a bit and those that had just landed. So I said, "I give up. Why does a bird peck at its feathers?"

"Because there are lice bothering it," he said. "The lice eat flakes of protein that come off its feathers." He continued, "Each louse has some waxy stuff on its legs, and little mites eat that. The mites don't digest it perfectly, so they emit from their rear ends a sugar-like material in which bacteria grow." Finally he said, "So you see, everywhere there's a source of food, there's some form of lice that finds it."

Now, I knew that it may not have been exactly a louse, that it might not be exactly true that the louse's legs have mites. That whole story about lice and mites was probably incorrect in detail, but what he was telling me was right in principle. He was telling me not to worry about names but to observe carefully, make up a story that connects what I saw, and then compare the story again with what happens in the world.

Journal

Write a story in which you try to present a main principle or lesson.

This is typical of children's stories. An example is the race between the tortoise and the rabbit. The tortoise is slow but always keeps moving. The rabbit is fast but stops and falls asleep, so he loses the race. The main principle is that consistent work can overcome a lack of talent. Ask friends or parents for help on this.

_____

_____

_____

_____

_____

_____

_____

_____

_____

_____

_____

_____

_____

_____

_____

_____

_____

_____

_____

34

Where'd They Get That Idea? Volume 1

Two Different Kinds of Minds
by B. Pascal

Some people are good at mathematics. Their minds understand truths that are very simple, obvious, and clear. However, these are not the kinds of truths we come across in our daily, ordinary experience. And, because of our usual habits, it is hard to turn our attention to truths of this sort. Other sorts of people have minds that grasp the truths of their daily lives without thinking. They are quick to understand everyday things. They understand things by a kind of feeling. We call these people intuitive. These truths of experience are right in front of us, but only some people have eyesight sharp enough to see them all since there are so many. And if you miss any one of these truths, you'll make mistakes since they are all connected.

People who are good at mathematics are used to very exact and simple truths and rules. They do not reason well unless they can carefully arrange and order these truths. So they get lost when they try to think about their daily experience. That is because the rules of daily experience cannot be arranged and organized. We feel these truths of daily experience rather than think about them. Intuitive people seize a conclusion immediately rather than reach it through a process of reasoning. So it is very rare to find someone who is good at mathematics and also intuitive. People good at mathematics often appear silly because they try to think about their everyday experiences mathematically. They want to start with definitions and simple rules and reason from these. On the other hand, people who are intuitive and judge things at a glance are shocked when they look at a piece of mathematics. They cannot understand why one has to start with definitions and carefully reason step by step to a conclusion. So these two types of people could not be more different.

Worksheet #8

Individual Work

1. **Arrange the professions below according to whether you think they are more mathematical or intuitive.** Place them along the straight line indicating whether you think the professions are closer to being intuitive or to being mathematical, which are at opposite ends of the line.

Intuitive _____ Mathematical

Lawyers (L)   Doctors (D)
Musicians (Mu)   Historians (H)
Engineers (E)   Teachers (T)
Cooks (C)

2. **Are you mathematical or intuitive?** Place your initials on the straight line above to indicate where you think you belong. Explain why you placed yourself there.

_____

_____

_____

_____

_____

_____

Small Group Work

I. Appoint a chairperson and a secretary.

II. Compare your answers to question #1. Come up with one arrangement on which you all agree.

Intuitive _____ Mathematical

Journal

Why are some people afraid of mathematics?

_____

_____

_____

_____

_____

_____

_____

_____

_____

_____

_____

_____

_____

_____

_____

_____

_____

_____

_____

_____

_____

_____

_____

_____

Worksheet #9

Individual Work   **i**

1. What is the largest thing you have ever seen?

_____

_____

_____

2. Could it have been larger?

_____

_____

_____

3. Have you ever asked or been asked where the end of the universe is or how large it is? What do you think led you or the other person to ask this question?

_____

_____

_____

_____

Small Group Work   **S**

Appoint a chairperson and a secretary for your group.

I. How you would answer someone who asked where the end of the universe is?

_____

_____

_____

_____

_____

_____

On the Nature of Things
by Lucretius

Today we will talk about the universe. We all know what that is, don't we? It's everything: the trees, the oceans, and land here on the earth, the planets and the sun, the stars that we see at night, and all the empty space. Empty space is part of the universe too. We also ask how big is it. Does it just go on and on or does it end? I say that it goes on and on in every direction. It is not bounded anywhere. If the universe were bounded, then it would have an edge. But if there is an edge then there is something beyond it that makes it possible for us to see the edge. But the universe is everything, so this thing that we imagined beyond the edge must also be part of the universe. It doesn't matter where you stand in the universe or where you are, it goes on and on without any limit or edge or end in every direction. But this sounds hard to accept, so let us try to imagine the opposite. Let us try to imagine an edge or boundary to the universe, an end to all space. And let us now suppose that a person goes there with a spear and hurls it with all the force possible. What happens to the spear? It either goes on in the direction it was thrown or something stands in its way, stops it and sends it back in some other direction. But either of these possibilities forces you to confess that the universe goes on without end. If the spear continues, then it wasn't at the edge. If something stops it then what stops it was at the edge, so the spear wasn't thrown from the edge. Wherever you place the limit, you can ask what happens with the spear. When you do, you realize the universe can't have an end.

Journal

Do you think the universe goes on forever or does it stop somewhere? Why?

Worksheet #10

Individual Work

1. **Which class in school do you think changes you the most?** Which has the least effect on what you are like? From the list below, choose which class changes you the most and which changes you the least. Write your answers in the space provided.

Language Arts
Math   _____ Changes me the most.
Science
Social Studies
Physical Education   _____ Changes me the least.
Art
Music

2. **Explain your choices.**
    a) Class that changes you most:

    _____

    _____

    b) Class that changes you least:

    _____

    _____

Small Group Work

I. Form a group with three or four other students who had the same answer to "Which class in school do you think changes you the most?"

II. Appoint a chairperson and a secretary. As a group, **try and come up with five ways that studying mathematics could change a person.**

_____

_____

_____

_____

_____

_____

The Arithmetic
by Nicomachus of Gerasa

By studying numbers and arithmetic we change for the better. The thinking part of our minds begins to take control of us. It takes control over our feelings. We become less emotional. It enables us to order our emotions of anger and love. We hold our desires for things in check and we are better able to decide which ones are really good for us. The thinking part becomes sharp and powerful, and rules the confused emotions. We then become gentle, brave, and patient. Self-discipline and self-respect increase.

A Conversation Between
Abraham Lincoln and J. P. Gulliver
September 1, 1860
Reported by Gulliver

Lincoln: When I was studying law, I constantly came upon the word demonstrate. At first I thought I understood it, but soon realized that I did not. What do I mean when I demonstrate something more than when I reason about it or prove it? How does demonstration differ from proof? I checked the dictionary. According to it, demonstration was certain proof, a proof "beyond even the possibility of doubt". But I could form no idea of what sort of proof that was. I knew as much about it as a blind man about the color blue. At last I said to myself, "Lincoln, you'll never make a lawyer if you do not understand what demonstrate means." So I left my studies of the law and went to my father's house and began to study Euclid's *Book of Geometry*. I stayed there and studied this geometry book until I could present and demonstrate all the propositions. Then I knew what it was to demonstrate and could return to my law studies.

Gulliver: I hope you will allow me to use this fact publicly. No man can speak well unless he can define for himself what he is talking about. Euclid's *Book of Geometry*, if studied carefully, would cure the world of many of the evils in it. It would banish half the nonsense that now deludes and curses it. If only we could get people to read it.

44

Where'd They Get That Idea? Volume 1

Journal

In this lesson we have been considering how studying math could change you in other ways. How do you think a person who made the effort to really study math would change? What would that person be like in other things he or she does?

_____

_____

_____

_____

_____

_____

_____

_____

_____

_____

_____

_____

_____

_____

_____

_____

_____

_____

_____

Worksheet #11

Individual Work

1. **Using straight lines, try to divide the figures below into two symmetrical parts.** We have given you an example with an equilateral triangle. (An equilateral triangle has three sides that are all the same length.)

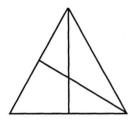

a. Equilateral Triangle

b. Isosceles Triangle

c. Square

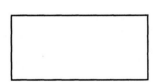

d. Rectangle

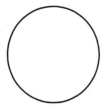

e. Circle

Small Group Work

I. **Compare your answers with the answers of the other members of your group.** As a group, decide how many different ways there are of cutting each figure into two symmetrical parts.

_____ Equilateral triangle

_____ Isosceles triangle

_____ Square

_____ Rectangle

_____ Circle

A Geometrical Theorem
by Euclid

How many times can two straight lines meet? You may remember this from studying definitions of straight lines in lesson #2 of Unit Two in this book or from your other math classes. There are only two possibilities. Two straight lines meet either once or not at all, in which case they are parallel. If two lines meet in two points then one or both of them must be curved.

Example:

We will use this fact to show another fact about lines.

Are lines EF and CD parallel?

This proof will require us to use symmetry and the above characteristics of straight lines to prove that two lines are parallel.

Given: Two straight lines, EF and CD, with a third line AB crossing both of them. When AB cuts these lines, angles 1, 2, 3, and 4 are created such that Angle 1=Angle 2 and Angle 3=Angle 4 (see diagram)

Prove: We are asked to determine if lines EF and CD will meet or if they are parallel.

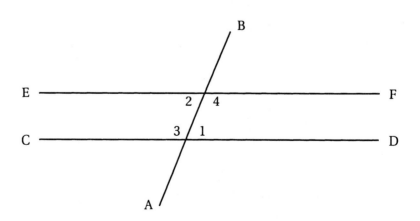

Proof: Let us imagine that lines EF and CD will meet. Towards which side will the lines meet? If we extend the lines to the right, they may meet at a point we will call W or if they extend to the left, they may meet at a point we will call Z. How do we decide?

First we have to recognize that the angles and lines on both sides of the crossing line AB are symmetrical. This is because of the equal angles listed above. Since these two halves are symmetrical, any reason we could give that the lines would meet at W must also mean that the lines would meet at Z.

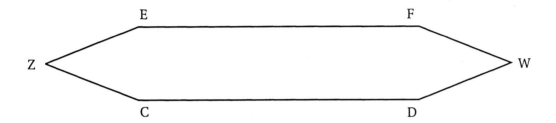

But we know that two straight lines cannot meet at two points.

Conclusion: So, we know that the straight lines EF and CD do not meet and, therefore, are parallel.

Journal

Did the proof convince you? Why or why not?

Worksheet #12

Individual Work

1. Suppose you are a doctor conducting experiments on the use of a drug to cure cancer. You are trying to figure out the right dose to use on humans and you know that using the wrong dose can be very dangerous. From the list below, decide which subjects you think it would be all right to use for experiments. Check the appropriate boxes. In addition, circle the one which you would most like to use for experiments.

    ❑   dogs

    ❑   people who volunteer

    ❑   monkeys

    ❑   mice

    ❑   people who are dying of cancer

    ❑   yourself and other scientists

Small Group Work

I. Form a group with three or four others who circled the same response as you. **Discuss and try to come to agreement on reasons why that is the best animal or subject to be experimented on.**

_____

_____

_____

_____

_____

_____

_____

Introduction to Experimental Medicine
by C. Bernard

Do we have the right to experiment on animals? As for me, I think we definitely have this right. It would be strange if we said that human beings have the right to use animals for food, but do not have the right to use them for learning things which are useful for preserving human life. You cannot deny that progress in medicine needs experiments. We can save some living beings from death only by killing others. Experiments must be made, either on human beings or on animals. If it is wrong to do experiments on human beings, then it must be right to do experiments on animals. This is true even if the experiments are painful and dangerous to the animal, as long as they are useful to human beings.

What about the objections of some serious people who are not scientists? They feel that experiments on animals are wrong because the animals suffer. They think the scientists who do these experiments are cruel. But what about a soldier who has to kill for his country, or a surgeon who must hurt someone in order to cure him? Are they also cruel? Are they like a person who enjoys hurting other people? I don't think so! What makes them different are the ideas they have. The doctor wants to cure disease. The soldier wants to protect his country. In the same way the medical scientist who does experiments on living animals wants to learn things. He is following his own scientific idea. He doesn't hear the cries of the animals or see the blood which is flowing. What other people find disgusting, he finds interesting. As long as he is under the influence of the scientific idea, nothing else matters very much to him. People who do not share his idea will think he is cruel, and he will not be able to convince them otherwise. He will be able to discuss what he does only with other scientists. Only his own conscience can tell him whether his actions are right or wrong.

Journal

1.   Was there a great deal of disagreement in this class discussion?

_____

_____

2.   Why do you this there was so much agreement or disagreement on this subject?

_____

_____

_____

_____

_____

_____

_____

_____

_____

_____

_____

_____

_____

_____

_____

_____

_____

_____

Worksheet #13

Individual Work

1. The diagram below contains a flashlight pointed towards a mirror and a wall. **Starting at the flashlight, draw a line to represent the path the light will travel from the flashlight and how it will reflect off the mirror.**

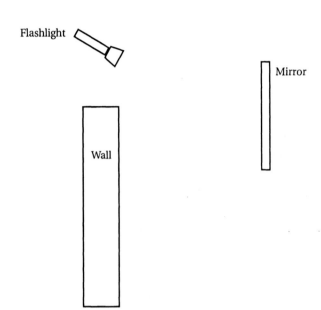

2. **How would you convince someone that the path you drew is the actual path the light would travel?** Write your answer below.

_____

_____

_____

_____

_____

_____

_____

_____

_____

Small Group Work

I. Compare your paths with the other members of your group. Decide on one path and one explanation for why the light would travel in that path.

_____

_____

_____

_____

_____

_____

_____

_____

_____

_____

_____

_____

_____

_____

_____

_____

_____

_____

Letter to Dr. Clarke
by G. W. Leibniz

The great principle of mathematics is the principle of non-contradiction or identity. This principle says that a statement cannot be both true and false at the same time and in the same way. Starting from this principle you can prove every theorem of mathematics. But in order to go from mathematics to science, another principle is needed. I call this the principle of sufficient reason. This principle states that nothing happens without a reason and that this reason will explain not only why an event happens but why it happens in that particular way.

Archimedes in his book *On Equilibrium* makes use of the principle of sufficient reason. He takes it for granted that, if there is a balance in which everything is the same on both sides and if equal weights are hung on the two ends of that balance, the whole will be at rest. He takes this for granted because if you cannot give a reason for a motion to take place, then it will not take place. All the principles of physics that have to do with forces and causes depend on this principle of sufficient reason.

Journal

Would it surprise you if equal weights at equal distances did not balance? Suppose this is what you saw. How would you explain it?

_____

_____

_____

_____

_____

_____

_____

_____

_____

_____

_____

_____

_____

_____

_____

_____

_____

_____

_____

_____

_____

Worksheet #14

Individual Work

i

Answer the following questions "Yes" or "No."

1. **Consider this line.**
   We can draw one twice as long,
   and then make that one twice as long.
   Can we keep doubling this line without ever having to stop?

   ☐ YES   ☐ NO

2. **Is there one line that is longer or as long as any other line?** (In other words, is there a line which is longer than any other line?)

   ☐ YES   ☐ NO

3. **Can any number be doubled?**

   ☐ YES   ☐ NO

4. **Is there a number that is as large or larger than any other number?** (In other words, is there a number which is greater than any other number?)

   ☐ YES   ☐ NO

Small Group Work

S

I. **Consider lines which are very short.** Is there a line so short that even if we looked at it under a very powerful magnifying glass we would see that it couldn't be made shorter?

   ☐ YES   ☐ NO

II. **Draw the shortest line you can and use the magnifying glass to look at it.**

Physics
by Aristotle

It is plain that an actual thing cannot be infinite. For if we take away a part of the infinite, what is left is still infinite. This will happen whatever the size of the part, even if the part is itself infinite. But this is absurd since then the part of the infinite is itself infinite. The whole would be the same size as part of it. Therefore the infinite cannot have parts. But it must if it is complete and actually infinite. For everything that is complete has parts. So the infinite cannot be an actual thing.

But to believe that the infinite doesn't exist in any way leads to many impossible conclusions. It would mean that a line couldn't be made longer or that we couldn't keep dividing a line. It would also mean that there would only be so many numbers. But what is left? If we require some sort of infinite and it cannot be an actual thing, it must be a potential thing. We talk about things in two ways—as actual and as potential. The table we sit next to is an actual table. The wood in the storage room in the carpenter's shop is a potential table. When the carpenter finishes working on it, it is an actual table. Now we see that the infinite cannot be an actual thing. And since we require some sense of the infinite it must be a potential thing. But it is potential in an unusual way. The wood that is a potential table can become an actual table when the carpenter builds it. But the potential infinite can never become an actual infinite; the line only becomes longer or the numbers larger.

60

Where'd They Get That Idea? Volume 1

Journal

Based on the class discussion, would you change any of your answers from the activity? Explain your answers. Use the back of this page if you need more room.

1. **Consider this line.**
    We can draw one twice as long,
    and then make that one twice as long.
    Can we keep doubling this line without ever having to stop?

    ☐ YES   ☐ NO

2. **Is there one line that is longer or as long as any other line?** (In other words, is there a line which is longer than any other line?)

    ☐ YES   ☐ NO

3. **Can any number be doubled?**

    ☐ YES   ☐ NO

4. **Is there a number that is as large or larger than any other number?** (In other words, is there a number which is greater than any other number?)

    ☐ YES   ☐ NO

_____

_____

_____

_____

_____

_____

_____

_____

_____

_____

_____

_____

Lesson

Worksheet #15

Individual Work

i

We often try to convince others of something we believe. Have you ever had a disagreement with a friend about what was the best tasting food, TV show, singer, or basketball team? This has happened to all of us and there are different ways we use to try to convince someone we are right. Usually I try to find things I know they agree with and then use these to convince them about what we are now discussing. But you may do it in different ways. Some people like to show that a certain opinion is so silly that its opposite must be true.

1. **Suppose you are going to try to convince someone to agree with you.** Which of the topics listed below would be the easiest to convince someone to agree with you about? Mark that one with an "E". Which would be the hardest? Mark that one with an "H". Explain why you think it would be hard to convince the other person to agree with you about the one you marked "H".

   _____ Best TV show   _____ Best tasting food

   _____ Best song   _____ Best singing group

   _____ Best thing to do when angry with someone

2. **How would you try to convince the other person?** Would you try to show them that their choice does not make sense and therefore you are right? Or would you try to show them why you are right and therefore they must be wrong? Choose one approach and explain why.

   _____

   _____

   _____

   _____

   _____

Small Group Work

I.   As a group, decide which of the two proofs you like better.

Two Proofs of the Same Truth

We are going to look at two different kinds of proofs of the same statement. We will try to prove that the diameter of a circle equals two times the radius. In the circle ABCD, we will try to prove that the diameter BWD equals two times the radius WD.

First we need some definitions.

> **Circle.** A circle is a figure like ABCD in which every point on the circumference ABCD is the same distance from one point inside the circle. In this case the point W.

> **Radius.** A radius is the distance from point W to the circumference, for example the line WA is a radius.

> **Diameter.** A diameter is a straight line that passes through point W and touches the circle in two points. In figure 1, the lines AWC and BWD are diameters.

Proof 1 (direct proof)

1. BWD is a diameter.

2. BWD=BW+WD.

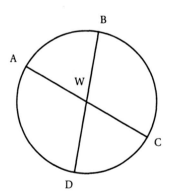

3. Because ABCD is a circle
   and BW and WD are lines from point W
   to the circumference, they are equal.

4. So BW=WD and each is a radius.

5. So BWD=WD+WD=2WD or twice the radius WD.

64

Where'd They Get That Idea? Volume 1

Proof 2 (indirect proof)

1. Suppose in circle ABCD the diameter BWD
   were not equal to twice the radius WD.

2. But diameter BWD=BW+WD.

3. So BW would not equal WD.

4. But WD and BW are lines from the point W to the circumference.

5. Then since they are not equal, the figure ABCD would not be a circle.

6. But we assumed ABCD was a circle, so this conclusion is absurd.

7. Therefore it must be wrong that diameter BWD does not equal twice the radius WD.

8. Therefore BWD equals twice the radius WD.

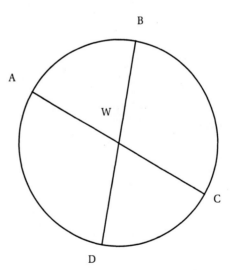

Journal

Below are a variety of circles. **If you took a ruler and measured the radius and diameter in each one and discovered that in each circle the diameter was two times the radius, would you believe this would be true of all circles?** How many circles of different sizes would you want to try before you completely believed it?

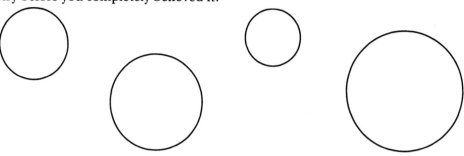

Do you need a proof like the one in the text to know that this would be true of all circles? Why or why not?

_____

_____

_____

_____

_____

_____

_____

_____

_____

_____

_____

_____

_____

_____

_____

_____

Common Ideas from *The Elements*
by Euclid

1. Things which are equal to the same thing are also equal to one another.

   Suppose A=B and B=C, then A=C.

2. If equals are added to equals, the sums are equal.

   Suppose A=B and C=D, so A+C=B+D.

3. If equals are subtracted from equals, the remainders are equal.

   Suppose A=B and C=D, so A-C=B-D.

4. Things which fit exactly on one another are equal to one another.

5. The whole is greater than the part.

   A+B is greater than A.

Worksheet #16

Individual Work

1. The list below has a few common notions from the text and one that was not in the text. After each one, write how true you think it is using the scale below. Is it true of everything, many things, few things, nothing?

    Always True   = 4
    Usually True   = 3
    Sometimes True = 2
    Rarely True   = 1
    Never True   = 0

    _____ a) **Things which are equal to the same thing are also equal to one another.**
    If A=B and B=C then A=C.

    _____ b) **If equals are added to equals, the sums are equal.**
    If A=B and C=D, then A+C=B+D.

    _____ c) **The whole is greater than the part.**
    A+B is greater than A.

    _____ d) **A thing is equal to itself.**
    A=A.

2. Do you think most students in your class would agree with your choices?

    ❏ YES   ❏ NO

3. Write down an opinion you think everyone in your class believes. This can be about anything and should not be one of those listed above.

    _____

    _____

    _____

    _____

Small Group Work

I. Appoint a chairperson and a secretary.

II. Look at the two notions that received the highest score. Imagine a situation in which those notions are not true, or not clearly true, and write it below.

_____

_____

_____

_____

_____

_____

_____

_____

_____

_____

_____

_____

_____

_____

_____

_____

_____

_____

Journal

1. **Write down something you think is absolutely true.** A test of this is that no one could persuade you it was false.

_____

_____

_____

_____

_____

_____

_____

_____

_____

2. **Write down something you think is absolutely false.** A test would be that no one could convince you that it is true.

_____

_____

_____

_____

_____

_____

_____

_____

_____

_____

Worksheet #17

Lesson 17

Individual Work

i

1. Are all inventions useful? Explain your answer.

_____

_____

_____

_____

_____

2. Do scientists have any responsibility for how their discoveries are used? Explain your answer.

_____

_____

_____

_____

_____

3. If you discovered a fact that was painful or dangerous to people, would you automatically tell them or consider keeping it secret? For example, if you discovered that the earth was getting closer to the sun and that all life would be threatened, what would you do?

_____

_____

_____

_____

_____

Small Group Work

S

I. Discuss your answers to all three questions with the other members of your group.

The Value of Science
by Henri Poincaré

The search for truth should be the goal of our activities. No other goal is worthy of us.

But truth can sometimes frighten us. It is sometimes deceptive. It is a phantom which shows itself for a moment only to flee endlessly from our grasp. And truth is also cruel. And one could argue that illusion is preferable. Illusions can console us, for they give us confidence. If illusion vanishes, will hope remain, and will we still have the courage to act? For example, the horse harnessed to the treadmill would refuse to budge if his eyes were not covered. However, we shouldn't listen to any of this. This only shows us that to seek truth we must be independent and brave.

First, by truth I mean scientific truth, but I also mean to include moral truth. It may seem that I misuse words by calling both of these truth. They have nothing in common. Scientific truth is demonstrated, moral truth is felt. But I can't separate them; anyone who loves one, loves the other. To find either, the soul must be completely free of prejudice and emotions. Our souls must attain absolute sincerity. We shouldn't fear moral truth, and we shouldn't dread scientific truth. First of all, they can't conflict. Science and morality have their own regions, which touch but don't overlap. Morality shows us the goals we should have, science teaches us how to attain them. They never conflict since they never meet. There cannot be immoral science, any more than there can be a scientific morality.

When we fear science, it is primarily because it cannot give us happiness. We are attracted by the image of the contented animal who seems to suffer less than man. We cannot be happy through science, but today we would be less happy without it.

72

Where'd They Get That Idea? Volume 1

Journal

Do you feel that we should learn truth at all costs? Or do you think there are certain truths it would be better for us not to know? What would be such a truth and why is it better for us not to know it?

_____

_____

_____

_____

_____

_____

_____

_____

_____

_____

_____

_____

_____

_____

_____

_____

_____

_____

_____

_____

Worksheet #18

Individual Work

Below are some definitions of a square and a circle and a straight line. Under these you will find a number of figures.

1.   For the first three figures, write down why they are or are not really circles.

2.   For the next group of three figures, write down why they are or are not really squares.

A **circle** is a single line all of whose points are the same distance from one point inside called the center.

A **line** whether curved or straight has length but no width.

A **square** is a figure that has four equal straight lines as its sides, and four equal angles.

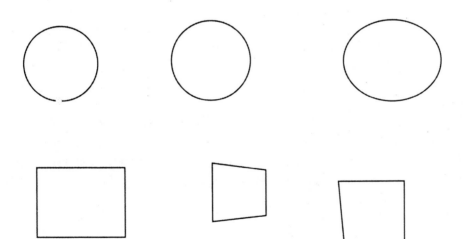

Small Group Work

I.   As a group, discuss your answers to questions 1 and 2 of the Individual Work.

The Republic
by Plato

You know that when people study geometry they look at pictures and drawings of triangles and lines and squares. They even talk about these figures while looking at these diagrams. But they are not talking about the figures they see drawn. These figures are like shadows and reflections in water of the real triangles and squares. These real triangles and squares can only be seen by our minds. The ones we draw are useful because they help us grasp what we can never see with our eyes.

Geometry and Experience
by A. Einstein

This is the riddle that has puzzled people throughout the ages. Geometry is entirely a product of our minds. So how is it possible for geometry to be in such perfect agreement with the objects in the world? How can it be that the images of triangles and straight lines we form through our imaginations can be used to measure things that our minds didn't create but that we find in the world? Is it because without any experience our minds give us information about the world? My answer is NO. We can apply geometry to the world because we discovered that the rulers which are most useful for measuring things look very much like the straight lines in our geometry books. But this is a fact we had to discover. It could have been different. If it turned out that the shortest distance between two places in a room we were measuring looked like a curved line and not a straight line, then our rulers would be very different. This is exactly what happens when we measure distances on a globe, like the earth. Or it might be that nothing in the world corresponded to the straight lines in our geometry books and then we would not be able to talk about the length of something.

Journal

Do you think numbers or triangles and straight lines are more useful to us in our everyday activities? Mention a few ways you use them everyday. What would your life be like if we could use neither geometry nor arithmetic? For example, if every time you counted the change in your pocket, you got a different amount.

Printed in the United States
203019BV00006B/161-412/A

9 781878 461490